PUBLISHED BY ROBERT CORBIN

Low Food-map: the Ultimate Guide

Delicious Recipes to Soothe Your Gut

@ Garry Tidd

Published By Robert Corbin

@ Garry Tidd

Low Food-map: the Ultimate Guide

Delicious Recipes to Soothe Your Gut

All Right RESERVED

ISBN 978-87-94477-95-6

TABLE OF CONTENTS

berry Muffins 1

Vegetable Frittata 4

Hard-Boiled Eggs 6

Yogurt Parfait 7

Greek Salad 8

Baked Cod With Lemon And Herbs: 10

Vegetable Soup 12

Scrambled Tofu Breakfast: A Nourishing Way To Start Your Day 14

Gluten-Free Tortilla With Low-Fodmap: A Delightful Morning Meal 16

Indigo Berry Breakfast Bowl 17

Breakfast Fruit Salad 19

Banana Split Oatmeal 21

Egg Tacos With Avocado 22

Chia Seed Breakfast Bowl 23

Spinach And Feta Stuffed Chicken Breast 25

Cheddar Waffles With Bacon & Chives 26

Cornmeal Berry Snack Cake 32

Banana Chocolate Chip Muffins 36

Sweet Potato-Black Bean Burgers 39

Zucchini Noodles With Pesto & Chicken 42

Lemon-Shallot Dressing 45

Chia Pudding With Almond Milk, Cocoa Powder, And Walnuts 46

Toast With Nut Butter And Banana Slices 48

Apple-Cinnamon Oatmeal With Almond Milk 49

Stir-Fry With Vegetables And Shrimp: 51

Grilled Swordfish With Herb Marinade: 53

Poached Cod With Herbed Tomato Broth: 55

Blueberry Overnight Oats 57

Tofu Scramble 59

Quinoa Salad With Roasted Vegetables 61

Tofu Zucchini Rice Bowl 63

Salad With Fody 65

Turkey Sandwich 66

Low Fodmap Salad 67

Low Fodmap Leftovers	69
Low Fodmap Smoothie	70
Quinoa And Vegetable Stir-Fry	71
Spinach And Tomato Frittata	73
Chicken And Vegetable Curry	75
Delicious Strawberry Chia Pudding	77
Banana Peanut Butter Toast	79
Quick And Easy Low-Fodmap Smoothie Recipe	80
Crispy Hash Brown With Egg	81
Grilled Almond Butter Banana Sandwich	83
Avocado-Cheese Bagel	84
Almond Butter And Banana Overnight Oats	85
Greek Yoghourt Parfait With Granola And Berries	87
Rice Cracker "Sandwiches" With Turkey And Lettuce	88
Chia Pudding	90
Indonesian Black Rice Pudding	92
Breakfast Bars	95
Garlic Roasted Salmon & Brussels Sprouts	99

Easy Salmon Cakes With Arugula Salad 101

Broccoli & Cauliflower Casserole 104

Grilled Chicken With Roasted Vegetables 107

Chicken And Rice Soup 109

Herb-Crusted Baked Chicken 111

Lemon Garlic Shrimp Stir-Fry 113

Baked Lemon Dijon Salmon 115

Shrimp With Spicy Garlic 117

Lentil And Vegetable Curry 119

Quinoa Breakfast Bowl 122

Greek Salad 124

Pasta Salad 126

Chicken Wrap 129

Ground Beef Tacos 132

Low Fodmap Sandwich 133

Low Fodmap Wrap 135

Grilled Steak With Roasted Potatoes 136

Capers Salad 138

Lemon Herb Roasted Chicken Thighs 140

Berry Muffins

Ingredients:

- 1/2 cup granulated sugar
- 2 teaspoons baking powder
- 1/2 teaspoon baking soda
- 1/4 teaspoon salt
- 1/2 cup lactose-free milk (e.g., almond milk, rice milk)
- 1/4 cup melted coconut oil
- 2 large eggs
- 1 1/2 cups gluten-free all-purpose flour
- 1/2 cup almond flour
- 1 teaspoon vanilla extract

- 1 cup fresh berries (e.g., blueberries, raspberries, strawberries)

Directions:
1. Turn on the oven to 350 °F (175 °C). Use paper liners to line a muffin pan or lightly oil the cups.
2. The gluten-free all-purpose flour, almond flour, granulated sugar, baking powder, baking soda, and salt should all be thoroughly blended in a large mixing basin.
3. The lactose-free milk, melted coconut oil, eggs, and vanilla extract should all be thoroughly combined in a different bowl.
4. After adding the liquid components, mix the dry Ingredients: only until they are barely blended. Avoid over mixing; the batter should still have some lumps.
5. Fresh berries should be gently incorporated into the batter.

6. Fill each cup in the muffin tin about two-thirds full with the batter.
7. A toothpick put into the center of a muffin should come out clean after baking the muffins in the preheated oven for 18 to 20 minutes.
8. The muffins should be taken out of the oven and given some time to cool in the pan. After that, move them to a wire rack to finish cooling.

Vegetable Frittata

Ingredients:

- 1/2 cup chopped zucchini
- 1/4 cup chopped spinach
- 6 eggs
- 1/4 cup milk
- 1/4 teaspoon salt
- 1/4 teaspoon black pepper
- 1 tablespoon olive oil
- 1/2 cup chopped onion
- 1/2 cup chopped red bell pepper
- 1/4 cup grated Parmesan cheese

Directions:

1. oven to 350 degrees Fahrenheit (175 degrees Celsius).
2. In a sizable oven-safe skillet, warm olive oil over medium heat. Cook the zucchini, bell pepper, and onion for about 5 minutes or until tender.
3. Add the spinach and stir; cook for 1 minute, or until wilted.
4. Whisk the eggs, milk, salt, and pepper in a sizable basin.
5. When the eggs are set, about 10 minutes, pour the egg mixture into the skillet with the vegetables and simmer, stirring regularly.
6. Sprinkle with Parmesan cheese, then bake in a preheated oven for about 5 minutes, or until the cheese is melted and bubbling.
7. Before slicing and serving, allow it to cool slightly.

Hard-Boiled Eggs

Ingredients:

- 2 large eggs

Directions:

1. Place the eggs in a single layer in a saucepan.
2. Cover the eggs with cold water.
3. Bring the water to a boil.
4. Cover the pan and remove it from the heat.
5. Let the eggs stand in the hot water for 10 minutes.
6. Drain the hot water and run cold water over the eggs until they are cool to the touch.
7. Peel the eggs and serve.

Yogurt Parfait

Ingredients:

- 1/4 cup low fodmap berries
- 1 tablespoon low fodmap granola
- 1/2 cup low fodmap yogurt
- 1 tablespoon low fodmap nuts or seeds

Directions:

1. Layer the yogurt, berries, granola, and nuts or seeds in a glass or jar.
2. Serve immediately or refrigerate for later.

Greek Salad

Ingredients:

- Romaine lettuce
- Cucumber
- Cherry tomatoes
- Kalamata olives
- Feta cheese
- Olive oil
- Red wine vinegar
- Dried oregano
- Salt and pepper

Directions:

1. Chop romaine lettuce, cucumber, cherry tomatoes, and kalamata olives.

2. Crumble feta cheese.
3. Olive oil, red wine vinegar, dried oregano, salt, and pepper should all be combined in a bowl.
4. Toss the chopped vegetables, olives, and feta cheese with the dressing.
5. Serve the Greek salad as a side dish or add grilled chicken for a complete meal.

Baked Cod With Lemon And Herbs:

Ingredients:

- Lemon
- Fresh dill
- Garlic-infused olive oil
- Cod fillets
- Salt and pepper

Directions:

1. Preheat the oven to 375°F (190°C).
2. Cod fillets should be placed in a baking dish.
3. Drizzle the fillets with garlic-infused olive oil.
4. Squeeze lemon juice over the fillets.
5. Sprinkle with fresh dill, salt, and pepper.
6. Fish should be opaque and flake easily after baking for 15 to 20 minutes.

7. Serve the baked cod with steamed vegetables or a side salad.

Vegetable Soup

Ingredients:

- Green beans
- Red bell pepper
- Vegetable broth (check for FODMAP-friendly Ingredients:)
- Garlic-infused olive oil
- Fresh herbs (such as parsley or basil)
- Carrots
- Zucchini
- Salt and pepper

Directions:

1. Peel and chop carrots into small pieces.

2. Cut zucchini, green beans, and red bell pepper into bite-sized pieces.
3. Heat garlic-infused olive oil in a pot.
4. Add the chopped vegetables and sauté for a few minutes.
5. Pour vegetable broth into the pot, enough to cover the vegetables.
6. Simmer until the vegetables are tender.
7. Stir in fresh herbs, salt, and pepper.
8. Serve the low FODMAP vegetable soup hot.

Scrambled Tofu Breakfast: A Nourishing Way To Start Your Day

Ingredients:

- 1 cup of spinach
- 1/2 tsp of ground turmeric
- Salt and pepper to taste
- 2 slices of gluten-free bread
- 8 oz of firm tofu, crumbled and drained
- 1 red bell pepper, diced
- 1 green bell pepper, diced
- Fresh fruit of your choice for serving

Directions:

1. Start by heating a non-stick skillet over medium heat.

2. Add the crumbled tofu to the skillet and sauté it for 2-3 minutes until it takes on a light golden brown color.
3. Incorporate the diced bell peppers into the skillet and continue sautéing for an additional 2-3 minutes until the peppers soften.
4. Add the spinach and ground turmeric to the skillet, ensuring that the tofu is evenly coated with the vibrant yellow spice. Sauté until the spinach wilts.
5. Season the mixture with salt and pepper according to your taste preferences.
6. While the tofu scramble is cooking, toast the gluten-free bread slices until they turn a beautiful golden brown.
7. Serve the delectable scrambled tofu alongside the toasted gluten-free bread and some fresh fruit.

Gluten-Free Tortilla With Low-FODMAP: A Delightful Morning Meal

Ingredients:

- 1/4 cup of bell peppers, diced
- 2 slices of turkey bacon, chopped
- 1/4 cup of cheddar cheese, shredded
- 1 tablespoon of olive oil
- 1 gluten-free tortilla
- 2 large eggs
- Salt and pepper, to taste

Directions:
1. In a small bowl, whisk the eggs and season with salt and pepper. Set aside.
2. Heat the olive oil in a non-stick skillet over medium heat. Add the diced bell peppers and

cook until they soften, approximately 2-3 minutes.
3. Add the chopped turkey bacon to the skillet and cook until it turns crispy, approximately 2-3 minutes.
4. Pour the beaten eggs into the skillet and scramble until they are fully cooked.
5. Warm the gluten-free tortilla in the microwave for 10-15 seconds, or until it becomes soft and pliable.
6. Place the scrambled eggs, bell peppers, and turkey bacon in the center of the tortilla.
7. Sprinkle the shredded cheddar cheese on top.
8. Fold the sides of the tortilla inward, then roll it tightly to form a burrito.
9. Serve immediately.

Indigo Berry Breakfast Bowl

Ingredients:

- 1 ripe banana, peeled and cut into slices

- 1/2 cup of lactose-free yogurt

- 1/4 cup of unsweetened almond milk

- 1 cup of frozen indigo berries

- 1/4 cup of gluten-free oats

Directions:

1. Combine the frozen indigo berries, banana slices, lactose-free yogurt, and almond milk in a blender. Blend on high until the mixture becomes smooth and creamy.
2. Pour the blended smoothie into a bowl.
3. Garnish the breakfast bowl with gluten-free oats and more banana slices.
4. Serve immediately.

Breakfast Fruit Salad

Ingredients:

- 1 medium cantaloupe, skin removed and cubed
- 1 medium papaya, skin-removed and cubed
- 1 tablespoon lemon juice
- 1 tablespoon stevia (optional)
- 1 can pineapple chunks
- 2 large firm bananas, cubed
- ⅓ cup orange juice (optional)

Directions:
1. Mix all fruits in a bowl.
2. Boil your orange juice, lemon juice, and stevia in a small pot (over high heat). Stir well.

3. Let the juice be cooled. Then, add your cooled juice to the fruit bowl. Enjoy!

Banana Split Oatmeal

Ingredients:

- ½ cup water, almond milk or lactose-free milk
- 1 cup old-fashioned rolled oats or a small ready oatmeal package
- ½ banana, cubed
- Salt to taste

Directions:
1. Boil your milk or water in a pot over high heat.
2. Add oat and salt to it. Stir for two more minutes.
3. Serve your oatmeal with cubed bananas. Enjoy!

Egg Tacos With Avocado

Ingredients:

- 2 organic, free-range eggs
- ½ avocado
- 4 small gluten-free tortillas
- Salt to taste

Directions:
1. Warm or toast tortillas.
2. Scramble or boil your eggs using salt.
3. Mash your avocado
4. Fill your tortillas with avocado and eggs. Enjoy!

Chia Seed Breakfast Bowl

Ingredients:

- Low-FODMAP fruits (e.g., strawberries, blueberries, kiwi)
- Low-FODMAP granola
- Nuts or seeds (e.g., pumpkin seeds, almonds)
- Chia seeds
- Lactose-free yoghurts or coconut yoghourt
- Maple syrup (optional)

Directions:

1. In a bowl, mix 2-3 tablespoons of chia seeds with lactose-free yoghurts. Stir well and let it sit for at least 15 minutes or overnight to thicken.

2. Once the chia pudding has thickened, layer it with sliced low-FODMAP fruits like strawberries, blueberries, and kiwi.
3. Sprinkle a handful of low-FODMAP granola over the fruits for added crunch.
4. Top with a small handful of nuts or seeds for extra texture and a drizzle of maple syrup if desired.
5. Mix everything and enjoy your chia seed breakfast bowl!

Spinach And Feta Stuffed Chicken Breast

Ingredients:

- Lactose-free feta cheese
- Olive oil
- Lemon juice
- Herbs and spices (e.g., oregano, thyme, garlic-infused oil)
- Chicken breast
- Fresh spinach
- Salt and pepper

Directions:
1. Preheat the oven to 375°F (190°C).
2. Butterfly the chicken breast by slicing it horizontally, leaving one side intact.

3. In a skillet, sauté fresh spinach with a drizzle of olive oil until wilted. Let it cool slightly.
4. Mix the cooked spinach with crumbled lactose-free feta cheese, a splash of lemon juice, and your choice of herbs and spices.
5. Fill the chicken breast pocket with the mixture of spinach and feta, and use toothpicks to secure if necessary.
6. Add salt, pepper, and a bit of garlic-infused oil to season the chicken.
7. On medium-high heat, sear the chicken in an oven-safe skillet until it turns golden brown on both sides.
8. Then, place the skillet in the preheated oven and bake for approximately 15-20 minutes, ensuring the chicken is fully cooked.
9. Remove the toothpicks, slice the stuffed chicken breast, and serve with a side salad or roasted vegetables.

Cheddar Waffles With Bacon & Chives

Ingredients:

Waffles:

- 1 ½ teaspoons baking powder (gluten-free if following a gluten-free diet)
- 1 teaspoon salt
- ½ teaspoon baking soda
- Heaping ¼ teaspoon chipotle chile powder
- Heaping ⅛ teaspoon ground cumin
- Heaping ⅛ teaspoon oregano
- Pinch of cayenne
- 2 large eggs, at room temperature
- 2 tablespoons of unsalted butter, melted and cooled slightly
- 2 cups (480 ml) of lactose-free whole milk, at room temperature

- 2 teaspoons lemon juice

- 1 ⅓ cup (194 g) low FODMAP, gluten-free all-purpose flour, such as Bob's Red Mill Gluten Free 1 to 1 Baking Flour

- ½ cup (76 g) medium-grind yellow cornmeal

- ¼ cup (50 g) sugar

- 2 tablespoons Onion-Infused Oil, made with vegetable oil, plus extra

- 4 ounces (115 g) extra-sharp cheddar cheese, shredded

- ⅓ cup (24 g) minced fresh chives

Add-ons:

- Maple Syrup

- Thick-cut bacon, fried crisp and crumbled

- Poached or fried eggs

- Lactose-free sour cream

- Low FODMAP salsa

Directions:
1. Preheat the oven to 200°F (95°C).
2. In a medium-sized mixing bowl, whisk together the milk and lemon juice and let it thicken for 5 minutes.
3. In a large mixing bowl, whisk together the flour, cornmeal, sugar, baking powder, salt, baking soda, chipotle chile powder, cumin, oregano, and cayenne to aerate and mix, then set aside.
4. Whisk the eggs, melted butter, and 2 tablespoons of oil into the soured milk until combined. Pour this wet mixture over the dry Ingredients: and fold together until a few floury streaks remain. Fold in the shredded cheese and minced chives until the batter is completely blended.

5. Preheat the waffle iron according to the manufacturer's Directions:. Brush the waffle iron with a little additional Onion-Infused Oil.
6. Cook the waffles according to the manufacturer's directions until nicely browned. They may be slightly soft, but that's okay.
7. Transfer the cooked waffles to a rack in a heated oven while you cook the remaining waffles. The waffles will crisp up a little in the oven.
8. Serve the waffles immediately. They are delicious with maple syrup, bacon, and an egg on top.
9. You can also add a dollop of lactose-free sour cream, more chives, or chopped scallion greens. Low FODMAP salsa is a fantastic addition as well. Get ready to be wowed!
10. You can freeze the waffles in a zip-top bag and toast them directly from the freezer. No need

to thaw. Consider making a double batch and freezing some for later.

Cornmeal Berry Snack Cake

Ingredients:

- ⅔ cup (131 g) sugar, plus 2 tablespoons, divided

- 1 cup (145 g) low FODMAP, gluten-free all-purpose flour, such as Bob's Red Mill Gluten Free 1 to 1 Baking Flour

- ¾ cup (104 g) of medium-grind yellow cornmeal (finely ground cornmeal can be used)

- 2 teaspoons of baking powder (use gluten-free if following a gluten-free diet)

- ½ teaspoon of salt

- ½ cup (113 g; 1 stick) of unsalted butter, melted

- ¼ cup (60 ml) neutral-flavored vegetable oil, such as canola, rice bran, or blended vegetable oil

- ½ cup (120 ml) of lactose-free whole milk, at room temperature

- 2 teaspoons of lemon juice

- ½ cup (63 g) fresh blueberries, plus 2 tablespoons

- ½ cup (68 g) fresh raspberries, plus 2 tablespoons

- 2 large eggs, at room temperature

Directions:

1. Preheat the oven to 350°F (180°C) and position the rack in the center. Coat the interior of a 9-inch (23 cm) spring form pan with nonstick spray and set it aside.

2. In a large bowl, combine the milk and lemon juice, then let it sit for 5 minutes to thicken.
3. Meanwhile, place all of the berries in a non-reactive dish and sprinkle them with 2 tablespoons of sugar. Use a potato masher to gently smash the berries, and then set aside to allow the juices to release.
4. In a separate bowl, mix together the flour, cornmeal, baking powder, and salt to aerate and combine. Set aside.
5. Returning to the thickened, soured milk, whisk in the melted butter and oil.
6. Then whisk in the remaining ⅔ cup (131 g) of sugar and the eggs until everything is well blended and smooth.
7. Add the dry Ingredients: to the mixture and whisk until a few floury streaks remain.
8. Add about three-quarters of the berries and any released juices (you can estimate the amount), then switch to a silicone spatula and

fold all the Ingredients: together until well combined.

9. Scrape the batter into the prepared pan and sprinkle the remaining berries and their juices on top.
10. Bake for approximately 35 to 40 minutes, until the cake is golden brown and a toothpick inserted in the middle comes out clean.
11. Allow the cake to cool on a rack for 5 minutes, then remove it from the pan.
12. The cake can be enjoyed warm or at room temperature, and it is best served on the day it is baked, but leftovers can be wrapped in foil and stored at room temperature for a day or two.

Banana Chocolate Chip Muffins

Ingredients:

- 2 large eggs, at room temperature

- 3 small/medium (300 g) very ripe bananas

- 1 ½ cups (218 g) of low FODMAP gluten-free all-purpose flour, such as Bob's Red Mill 1 to 1 Gluten Free Baking Flour

- 1 teaspoon of baking soda

- ½ teaspoon of salt

- ½ cup (1 stick; 113 g) of unsalted butter, very soft, cut into pieces

- ⅔ cup (131 g) sugar

- 1 teaspoon of vanilla extract

- 5 ounces (140 g) mini semisweet chocolate chips, divided

Directions:

1. Preheat the oven to 350°F (180°C) and position the rack in the center.
2. Coat the interior of 12 muffin wells with nonstick spray or line them with fluted paper cups.
3. In a large mixing bowl, beat the butter and sugar with an electric mixer until light and fluffy, scraping down the bowl once or twice.
4. Beat in the vanilla extract, then beat in the eggs one at a time, ensuring each one is well mixed before adding the next.
5. Beat in the very soft, ripe bananas. The mixture may appear slightly curdled, but that's okay.
6. Sprinkle the flour, baking soda, and salt over the wet mixture and beat until a few floury streaks remain.

7. Add about three-quarters of the chocolate chips (you can estimate the amount) and beat until the batter is uniform.
8. Divide the batter into the prepared muffin wells and sprinkle additional chocolate chips on top of each uncooked muffin.
9. Bake for approximately 25 to 35 minutes, or until the muffins are puffy, golden brown, and a toothpick inserted in the middle comes out with a few moist crumbs attached.
10. Allow the pan(s) to cool on a rack for 5 minutes, then remove the muffins from the wells.
11. They are best enjoyed warm! Alternatively, you can cool them and store them in an airtight container at room temperature for up to 3 days. They can also be frozen in heavy-duty zip-top bags with the air removed for up to 1 month.

Sweet Potato-Black Bean Burgers

Ingredients:

- 1 teaspoon curry powder

- ⅛ teaspoon salt

- 1/2 cup plain unsweetened almond milk yogurt

- 2 tablespoons chopped fresh dill

- 2 tablespoons lemon juice

- 2 tablespoons extra-virgin olive oil

- 4 whole-wheat hamburger buns, toasted

- 2 cups grated sweet potato

- ½ cup old-fashioned rolled oats

- 1 cup no-salt-added black beans, rinsed

- ½ cup chopped scallions

- ¼ cup vegan mayonnaise

- 1 tablespoon no-salt-added tomato paste

- 1 cup thinly sliced cucumber

Directions:
1. Squeeze grated sweet potato with paper towels to
1. remove excess moisture; place in a large bowl.
2. Pulse oats in a food processor until finely ground; add to the bowl with the sweet potatoes.
3. Add beans, scallions, mayonnaise, tomato paste, curry powder and salt to the bowl; mash the mixture together with your hands. Shape into four 1/2-inch-thick patties.
4. Place the patties on a plate; refrigerate for 30 minutes.

5. Stir yogurt, dill and lemon juice together in a small bowl; set aside.
2. Heat oil in a large cast-iron skillet over medium-high heat. Add the patties; cook until golden brown, about 3 minutes per side.
3. Divide the yogurt sauce evenly among top and bottom bun halves. Top each bottom bun half with a burger and cucumber slices; replace top bun halves.

Zucchini Noodles With Pesto & Chicken

Ingredients:

- ¼ cup grated Parmesan cheese
- 1/4 cup plus 2 tablespoons extra-virgin olive oil, divided
- 2 tablespoons lemon juice
- 1 large clove garlic, quartered
- ½ teaspoon ground pepper
- 1 pound boneless, skinless chicken breast, cut into
- 4 medium-large zucchini (about 2 pounds), trimmed
- ¾ teaspoon salt, divided
- 2 cups packed fresh basil leaves

- ¼ cup pine nuts, toasted

- 1-inch pieces

Directions:

1. Using a spiral vegetable slicer, cut zucchini lengthwise into long, thin strands. Give the
2. strands a chop here and there so the noodles aren't too long. Place the zucchini in a colander and toss with 1/4 teaspoon salt. Let drain for 15 to
3. 30 minutes, then gently squeeze to remove any excess liquid.
4. Meanwhile, place basil, pine nuts, Parmesan, 1/4 cup oil, lemon juice, garlic, pepper and 1/4 teaspoon salt in a mini food processor. Process until almost smooth.
5. Heat 1 tablespoon oil in a large skillet over medium-high heat. Add chicken in one layer; sprinkle with the remaining 1/4 teaspoon salt.

6. Cook, stirring, until just cooked through, about 5 minutes. Transfer to a large bowl and stir in 3 tablespoons of the pesto.
7. Add the remaining 1 tablespoon oil to the pan.
8. Add the drained zucchini noodles and toss gently until hot, 2 to 3 minutes. Transfer to the bowl with the chicken. Add the remaining pesto and toss gently to coat.

Lemon-Shallot Dressing

Ingredients:

- 1 teaspoon honey
- ½ teaspoon salt
- ¼ teaspoon ground pepper
- 6 tablespoons extra-virgin olive oil
- 3 tablespoons lemon juice
- 2 tablespoons chopped shallot

Directions:
1. Whisk together oil, lemon juice, shallot, honey, salt and pepper in a small bowl.

Chia Pudding With Almond Milk, Cocoa Powder, And Walnuts

Ingredients:

- 1/3 cup white sugar
- 1/2 teaspoon ground cinnamon
- 1/4 teaspoon ground nutmeg
- 1/2 teaspoon pure vanilla extract
- 1 cup long grain white rice
- 3 cups almond milk
- 1/4 cup chopped almonds

Directions:
2. Preheat the oven to 350°F.
3. In a medium saucepan, combine the rice, almond milk, sugar, cinnamon, and nutmeg.

Bring to a boil over medium-high heat, stirring occasionally.
4. Reduce the heat to low and simmer, stirring occasionally, for 15 minutes.
5. Remove the pan from the heat and stir in the vanilla extract.
6. Pour the mixture into a 9-inch baking dish. Sprinkle the chopped almonds on top.
7. Bake for 35 minutes, or until the top is golden brown and the rice is tender.
8. Serve warm or at room temperature. Enjoy!

Toast With Nut Butter And Banana Slices

Ingredients:

- 2 slices of bread
- 2 tablespoons of nut butter
- 1 banana

Directions:

1. Preheat a toaster or toaster oven.
2. Spread one tablespoon of nut butter on each slice of bread.
3. Slice the banana and place it on top of the nut butter.
4. Place the slices of bread in the toaster or toaster oven and toast until golden brown.
5. Serve the toast warm. Enjoy!

Apple-Cinnamon Oatmeal With Almond Milk

Ingredients:

- 1/4 teaspoon ground nutmeg
- 1/4 teaspoon ground ginger
- U Pinch of salt
- 2 tablespoons chopped almonds
- 1 cup rolled oats
- 2 cups almond milk
- 1 medium apple, chopped
- 2 tablespoons brown sugar
- 1 teaspoon ground cinnamon
- 2 tablespoons dried cranberries

Directions:

1. In a medium saucepan, bring the almond milk to a boil over medium heat.
2. Add the oats, reduce the heat to low, and stir until thickened, about 5 minutes.
3. Add the apple, brown sugar, cinnamon, nutmeg, ginger, and salt.
4. Cook for 5 more minutes, stirring occasionally, until the apples are softened and the oats are creamy.
5. Remove from the heat and stir in the chopped almonds and dried cranberries.
6. Serve the oatmeal warm and enjoy!

Stir-Fry With Vegetables And Shrimp:

INGREDIENTS:

- 2 tablespoons low-sodium soy sauce (verify components are low in FODMAPs) one teaspoon of sesame oil

- 2 minced garlic cloves

- 1 tablespoon of ginger, grated

- 1 pound of peeled and deveined big shrimp

- 1 sliced red bell pepper 1 sliced zucchini 1 julienned carrot Sliced green onions (with only the green bits)

Directions:
1. The shrimp, low-sodium soy sauce, sesame oil, minced garlic, and grated ginger should all be combined in a bowl. Toss thoroughly to evenly coat the shrimp.

2. Give them 15 minutes to marinate.
3. a large skillet or wok should be heated to a high temperature.
4. When the shrimp are pink and opaque, add them to the skillet and cook for an additional two to three minutes. The shrimp should be taken out of the skillet and put aside.
5. Add the julienned carrot, zucchini, and red bell pepper to the same skillet.
6. Vegetables should be stir-fried for 4-5 minutes or until crisp-tender.
7. Add the cooked shrimp back to the skillet and stir everything around for another minute.
8. Serve the shrimp stir-fry with vegetables over steaming rice or rice noodles, garnished with thinly sliced green onions.

Grilled Swordfish With Herb Marinade:

Ingredients:

- two teaspoons of lemon juice, fresh
- 1 tablespoon chopped fresh parsley
- 1 tablespoon finely chopped fresh basil 1 tablespoon finely chopped fresh oregano pepper and salt as desired
- 4 steaks of swordfish
- Olive oil, two tablespoons

Directions:
1. Olive oil, lemon juice, parsley, basil, oregano, salt, and pepper should all be combined in a bowl.
2. The marinade should be poured over the swordfish steaks that have been placed in a

shallow dish. In the refrigerator, give them 30 minutes to marinate.
3. Set the grill's temperature to medium-high.
4. Swordfish steaks should be taken out of the marinade and grilled for three to four minutes on each side, or until done through and sporting grill marks.
5. Along with a sprinkling of fresh herbs and a squeeze of lemon juice, serve the grilled swordfish steaks.

Poached Cod With Herbed Tomato Broth:

Ingredients:

- 1 cup veggie broth (verify components are low in fodmaps) 2 minced garlic cloves

- 1 tablespoon freshly chopped basil, 1 tablespoon freshly chopped parsley, and 1

- Tablespoon freshly chopped dill

- 4 fillets of cod

- 1 can of diced tomatoes (14 ounces).

- Pepper and salt as desired

Directions:

1. Diced tomatoes, vegetable broth, minced garlic, chopped basil, parsley, dill, salt, and pepper should all be combined in a big skillet.

Over medium heat, bring the mixture to a simmer.
2. Make sure the cod fillets are well soaked in the liquid before placing them gently into the skillet.
3. Cod should be poached for 8 to 10 minutes, or until it is opaque and flakes with a fork, in a covered skillet.
4. Cod fillets should be taken out of the skillet and placed in small bowls with the herbed tomato broth spooned over them.
5. If desired, add more fresh herbs as a garnish.

Blueberry Overnight Oats

INGREDIENTS:

- 1 cup lactose-free milk (such as almond or rice milk)
- 1/2 cup fresh or frozen blueberries
- 2 tablespoons pure maple syrup
- 1 cup gluten-free rolled oats
- 1 tablespoon chia seeds

Directions:

1. In a jar or container, combine the rolled oats, lactose-free milk, blueberries, maple syrup, and chia seeds.
2. Stir well to mix all Ingredients: evenly.
3. Cover and refrigerate overnight.
4. In the morning, give it a good stir and add a splash of lactose-free milk if desired.

5. Serve chilled.

Tofu Scramble

Ingredients:

- 1/4 cup sliced scallions (green parts only)
- 1/2 teaspoon ground turmeric
- 1/2 teaspoon smoked paprika
- Salt and pepper to taste
- 8 ounces firm tofu, drained and crumbled
- 1/2 red bell pepper, diced
- 1 tablespoon olive oil

Directions:
1. Heat olive oil in a skillet over medium heat.
2. Add the crumbled tofu, diced bell pepper, and sliced scallions to the skillet.
3. Sprinkle with ground turmeric, smoked paprika, salt, and pepper.

4. Cook for about 10-12 minutes, stirring occasionally, until the tofu is lightly browned and heated through.
5. Adjust the seasoning if needed.
6. Serve hot as a breakfast scramble.

Quinoa Salad With Roasted Vegetables

Ingredients:

- 1 small eggplant, diced
- 8 cherry tomatoes, halved
- 2 tablespoons olive oil
- 1 tablespoon balsamic vinegar
- 1 tablespoon chopped fresh basil
- 1 cup cooked quinoa
- 1 medium zucchini, diced
- 1 red bell pepper, diced
- Salt and pepper to taste

Directions:
1. Preheat the oven to 400°F (200°C).

2. Spread the diced zucchini, red bell pepper, eggplant, and cherry tomatoes on a baking sheet.
3. Drizzle with olive oil and balsamic vinegar. Season with salt and pepper.
4. Roast for about 30-35 minutes, tossing halfway through, or until the vegetables are tender and slightly caramelized.
5. In a serving bowl, combine the roasted vegetables, cooked quinoa, and chopped fresh basil.
6. Toss gently to mix.
7. Serve at room temperature or chilled.

Tofu Zucchini Rice Bowl

Ingredients:

- 1-1/2 tsp ground ginger
- 1/4 cup rice wine
- 1/4 tsp Sriracha
- 1 tbsp sesame oil
- 1 tbsp vegetable oil
- 2 tsp sesame seeds
- 2 zucchini, halved and thinly sliced
- 14 oz extra firm tofu, pressed and cubed
- 1 tsp soy sauce
- 1 tsp fish sauce
- 2 cups cooked rice

Directions:

1. In a bowl, mix the rice wine, Sriracha, soy sauce, fish sauce, ginger, and other Ingredients:.
2. Toss the tofu in the mixture to coat. For ten to fifteen minutes, marinate.
3. In a sizable skillet or wok, warm the vegetable oil over medium heat.
4. When the tofu is fully cooked and golden brown, add it and continue to cook while stirring regularly. Take out of the pan and place aside.
5. To the same pan, add the sesame oil. Saute the sesame seeds for one minute, or until they begin to lightly roast.
6. Add the zucchini and simmer for 3 to 5 minutes, stirring periodically, until fork-tender.
7. To mix, return the tofu to the pan and toss. Over cooked rice, please.

Salad With Fody

Ingredients:

- 1 tomato, sliced
- 1/2 cup croutons
- 1/4 cup Fody Balsamic Vinaigrette dressing
- 1 head of romaine lettuce, chopped
- 1 cucumber, sliced
- Salt and pepper to taste

Directions:

1. In a large bowl, combine the lettuce, cucumber, tomato, and croutons.
2. Drizzle with the Fody Balsamic Vinaigrette dressing and season with salt and pepper to taste.
3. Toss to combine and serve.

Turkey Sandwich

Ingredients:

- 2 tablespoons low FODMAP mayonnaise
- 2 slices low FODMAP sliced turkey
- 1 slice (about 30 g) Swiss cheese
- Lettuce
- 2 slices low FODMAP bread
- Tomato slices

Directions:
1. On one side of each slice of bread, spread mayonnaise.
2. On one slice of bread, arrange the turkey, Swiss cheese, lettuce, and tomato.
3. Add the second slice of bread on top.
4. Slice in half, then relish!

Low Fodmap Salad

Ingredients:

- 1/4 cup low FODMAP red onion, chopped (avoid if high in fodmaps)
- 1/4 cup low FODMAP avocado, chopped
- 2 tablespoons low FODMAP olive oil
- 1 tablespoon low FODMAP balsamic vinegar
- 4 cups mixed low FODMAP greens, such as spinach, kale, and romaine lettuce
- 1/2 cup low FODMAP cucumber, chopped
- 1/2 cup low FODMAP tomatoes, chopped
- Salt and pepper to taste

Directions:

1. Combine the greens, cucumber, tomatoes, onion (if using), and avocado in a large bowl.
2. Whisk together the olive oil, balsamic vinegar, salt, and pepper in a small bowl.
3. Drizzle the dressing over the salad and toss to coat.
4. Serve immediately.

Low Fodmap Leftovers

Ingredients:

- 1 cup low FODMAP leftovers, such as grilled chicken, salmon, or roasted vegetables

Directions:
1. Heat the leftovers in a microwave or on the stovetop.
2. Serve with a side of low FODMAP rice, quinoa, or vegetables.

Low Fodmap Smoothie

Ingredients:

- 1/2 cup low FODMAP fruit, such as bananas, berries, or melons
- 1/4 cup low FODMAP greens, such as spinach or kale
- 1 cup low FODMAP milk or yogurt
- 1 tablespoon low FODMAP nut butter or seeds

Directions:
1. Blend all Ingredients: together until smooth.
2. Serve immediately.

Quinoa And Vegetable Stir-Fry

Ingredients:

- Carrots
- Red bell pepper
- Green onions (green parts only)
- Gluten-free soy sauce
- Sesame oil
- Quinoa
- Broccoli
- Salt and pepper

Directions:
1. Cook quinoa according to package Directions:.
2. Cut broccoli into small florets and slice carrots and red bell pepper into thin strips.

3. In a large skillet or wok, heat the sesame oil.
4. Add broccoli, carrots, and red bell pepper and stir-fry for a few minutes.
5. Add cooked quinoa and gluten-free soy sauce to the skillet.
6. Stir-fry until everything is well combined.
7. Season with salt and pepper.
8. Sprinkle with green onions before serving.

Spinach And Tomato Frittata

Ingredients:

- Cherry tomatoes
- Green onions
- Olive oil
- Eggs
- Spinach
- Salt and pepper

Directions:
1. Preheat the oven to 350°F (175°C).
2. Toss the eggs with salt and pepper after beating them in a bowl.
3. Heat olive oil in an oven-safe skillet.
4. Add spinach, cherry tomatoes, and green onions to the skillet.

5. Sauté until the spinach wilts and the tomatoes soften.
6. Over the veggies in the pan, pour the beaten eggs.
7. Cook until the edges are firm, about a few minutes.
8. Transfer the skillet to the preheated oven and bake for about 10-15 minutes or until the frittata is cooked through.
9. Serve the spinach and tomato frittata as a main dish or for brunch.

Chicken And Vegetable Curry

Ingredients:

- Green beans
- Coconut milk
- Low FODMAP curry paste
- Gluten-free soy sauce
- Garlic-infused olive oil
- Fresh cilantro
- Chicken breasts (cut into cubes)
- Bell peppers
- Carrots
- Salt and pepper

Directions:

1. In a large skillet heat the garlic-infused olive oil. Add chicken cubes and cook until browned.
2. Green beans, bell peppers, and carrots should all be cut into bite-sized pieces.
3. Add the vegetables to the skillet and sauté for a few minutes.
4. In a bowl, mix coconut milk, low FODMAP curry paste, gluten-free soy sauce, salt, and pepper.
5. Pour the sauce into the skillet and simmer until the chicken is cooked through and the vegetables are tender.
6. Garnish with fresh cilantro before serving.
7. Serve the chicken and vegetable curry over rice or quinoa.

Delicious Strawberry Chia Pudding

Ingredients:

- 1 cup of milk
- 1 tablespoon of maple syrup
- 1/2 cup of freshly sliced strawberries
- 1/4 cup of chia seeds
- 1 tablespoon of unsweetened coconut flakes (toasted)

Directions:

1. Take a small bowl and combine the chia seeds, lactose-free milk, and maple syrup. Ensure thorough mixing.
2. Gently incorporate the sliced strawberries into the mixture.

3. Cover the bowl with plastic wrap and refrigerate it overnight or for a minimum of 4 hours.
4. When you're ready to serve, remove the bowl from the refrigerator and give the pudding a gentle stir. Adjust the consistency by adding a little more lactose-free milk if desired.
5. Top the pudding with the remaining sliced strawberries and toasted coconut flakes.
6. Serve immediately and savor the delightful flavors!

Banana Peanut Butter Toast

Ingredients:

- 1/2 of a medium-sized banana, thinly sliced
- 1 teaspoon of honey
- 1 piece of gluten-free bread
- 1 tablespoon of all-natural peanut butter

Directions:
1. Toast the gluten-free bread until it turns a delicious golden brown.
2. Spread the all-natural peanut butter evenly on the toasted bread.
3. Place the thinly sliced banana on top of the peanut butter, arranging it in an even layer.
4. Drizzle the honey over the entire slice of toast.
5. Serve immediately.

Quick And Easy Low-FODMAP Smoothie Recipe

Ingredients:

- 1 cup of baby spinach
- 1 scoop of vanilla protein powder
- Ice (optional)
- 1 cup of lactose-free milk
- 1 cup of frozen strawberries

Directions:

1. Place lactose-free milk, frozen strawberries, baby spinach, and vanilla protein powder in a blender.
2. Blend all the Ingredients: until you achieve a smooth and creamy consistency. Add ice if desired.
3. Pour the mixture into a glass and enjoy immediately.

Crispy Hash Brown With Egg

Ingredients:

- ¼ cup gluten-free flour
- 2 tablespoons extra virgin olive oil
- 2 organic range-free eggs
- 2 large yellow potatoes, shredded
- Salt and pepper to taste

Directions:
1. Shred potatoes and rinse them until the water cleared. Dry potatoes.
2. Mix your potatoes with flour, eggs, salt, and pepper.
3. Flatten your mix in a large skillet and let it cook over medium heat until golden brown. Flip and cook the other side.

4. Remove from the skillet and drain with a paper towel. Enjoy!

Grilled Almond Butter Banana Sandwich

Ingredients:

- 1 banana
- 4 slices of gluten-free bread
- 1 tablespoon extra virgin olive oil
- Few grams of almond butter
- Maple syrup to taste

Directions:
1. Toast your bread slices, as you desired.
2. Mash banana, coat your bread with banana, almond butter, and maple syrup. Enjoy!

Avocado-Cheese Bagel

Ingredients:

- 1 white gluten-free bread, toasted
- 2 tablespoons lactose-free Swiss cheese
- ½ avocado, mashed
- Salt to taste

Directions:

1. Open the bagel and coat a half with cheese, avocado (mashed), and salt.
2. Cover with the other half. Enjoy!

Almond Butter And Banana Overnight Oats

Ingredients:

- Almond butter
- Banana (sliced)
- Chia seeds (optional)
- Gluten-free oats
- Lactose-free milk
- Cinnamon (optional)

Directions:

1. In a jar or container, combine 1/2 cup of gluten-free oats and 1 tablespoon of chia seeds (if using).
2. Pour in enough lactose-free milk to cover the oats.

3. Add a dollop of almond butter and a sprinkle of cinnamon (if desired).
4. Stir well, cover, and refrigerate overnight.
5. In the morning, top the oats with sliced banana and an extra drizzle of almond butter before enjoying.

Greek Yoghourt Parfait With Granola And Berries

Ingredients:

- Lactose-free Greek yoghourt
- Low-FODMAP granola
- Low-FODMAP berries (e.g., blueberries, strawberries)
- Maple syrup (optional)

Directions:

1. In a glass or bowl, layer lactose-free Greek yoghurt, a handful of low-FODMAP granola, and a layer of mixed berries.
2. Continue layering until the glass or bowl is filled.
3. Optionally, drizzle a touch of maple syrup over the top for added sweetness.
4. Mix the layers and savour the parfait!

Rice Cracker "Sandwiches" With Turkey And Lettuce

Ingredients:

- Lettuce leaves
- Dijon mustard (optional)
- Rice crackers
- Low-FODMAP deli turkey slices

Directions:
1. Lay out rice crackers on a plate.
2. Place low-FODMAP deli turkey slices on half of the crackers.
3. Top with fresh lettuce leaves and a drizzle of Dijon mustard if desired.
4. Press another rice cracker on top to create a "sandwich."

5. Repeat to make as many rice cracker sandwiches as desired and enjoy the savoury bites.

Chia Pudding

Ingredients:

For a single serving:

- 2 tablespoons plain yogurt
- ⅓ cup milk of your choice (oat, almond, dairy)
- ½ teaspoon maple syrup
- 2 tablespoons chia seeds
- A drop of vanilla extract

For a larger batch (4-6 servings):

- 2 cups milk of your choice (oat, almond, cow)
- 2 tablespoons maple syrup
- 1 teaspoon vanilla extract
- ½ cup chia seeds
- 1 cup plain yogurt

Directions:
1. In a jar or container, combine the chia seeds, yogurt, milk, maple syrup, and vanilla extract, and mix well to ensure all the Ingredients: are thoroughly combined.
2. Let the mixture sit on the countertop for about 10 minutes, then whisk again to break up any clumps and ensure the chia seeds are evenly distributed.
3. Screw a lid onto the jar or cover the container and place it in the refrigerator overnight or for at least 3 hours.
4. This resting time allows the chia seeds to absorb the liquid and create a pudding-like texture.
5. When you're ready to serve, give the chia pudding a final whisk to ensure a smooth consistency. Ladle it into bowls or glasses and add your preferred toppings, such as fresh fruit, nuts, or a drizzle of honey.

Indonesian Black Rice Pudding

Ingredients:

- 1 ½ cups water
- A pinch of salt
- 2 tablespoons coconut sugar or alternative sweetener (see notes)
- 1 cup Indonesian black rice
- 14 oz can full-fat coconut milk
- Chopped banana, coconut chips, and hemp hearts for garnish

Directions:

To make on the stovetop:

1. In a medium-sized saucepan, combine the black rice, coconut milk (keeping a couple of

teaspoons for drizzling if desired), salt, and 1 ½ cups of water.
2. Bring the mixture to a boil, then reduce the heat to low and simmer covered until the rice is soft and most of the liquid has been absorbed. This will take approximately an hour,then stir occasionally and monitor the cooking process.
3. Once the rice is cooked, remove the saucepan from the heat and whisk in one tablespoon of the sweetener.
4. Taste the pudding and adjust the sweetness if desired by adding more sweetener.

To make in the instant pot:
1. In the Instant Pot, combine the black rice, coconut milk, coconut sugar, and 1 cup of water.
2. Seal the Instant Pot and set it to Manual mode on High pressure for 22 minutes.

3. After the pressure cooking cycle is complete, allow the steam to naturally release for 10 minutes, then do a quick release to release the remaining steam.
4. Be cautious and use a kitchen towel or follow the manufacturer's Directions: for steam release.
5. Remove the lid and stir the rice pudding thoroughly.
6. Serve the pudding hot, warm, or chilled. Drizzle with additional coconut milk and garnish with sliced banana, coconut chips, and hemp hearts.

Breakfast Bars

Ingredients:

- ½ teaspoon baking soda
- ½ teaspoon salt
- 1 teaspoon pure vanilla extract
- 2 large eggs
- ½ cup 100% peanut butter
- ½ cup sugar
- 1 cup peanuts
- 1 cup low FODMAP chocolate chips
- 2 tablespoons olive oil
- 1.5 cups rolled oats (not instant)
- ¼ cup butter

- ½ cup low FODMAP flour
- ¼ cup pomegranate arils
- 1 teaspoon cinnamon
- ½ teaspoon baking powder

Directions:
1. Preheat the oven to 350 degrees Fahrenheit. Lightly butter a 9" x 13" baking dish and set it aside.
2. In a skillet, toast the olive oil and rolled oats over medium heat, stirring constantly, until you can smell the aroma. Transfer the toasted oats to a large bowl and let them cool.
3. In the same skillet, melt the butter and set it aside.
4. To the toasted oats, add the low FODMAP flour, pomegranate arils, cinnamon, baking powder, baking soda, and salt. Toss well to coat the Ingredients: with the flour.
5. In a separate bowl, combine the melted butter, vanilla extract, eggs, peanut butter, and sugar. Mix until smooth.
6. Add the wet mixture to the dry mixture and stir until well combined.

7. Stir in the peanuts and low FODMAP chocolate chips.
8. Transfer the mixture to the prepared baking dish and spread it out evenly using a rubber spatula.
9. Bake in the preheated oven for 18-20 minutes, or until the bars are golden brown.
10. Allow the bars to cool in the baking dish for at least 20 minutes before cutting them into bars.

Garlic Roasted Salmon & Brussels Sprouts

Ingredients:

- 1 teaspoon salt, divided
- ¾ teaspoon freshly ground pepper, divided
- 6 cups Brussels sprouts, trimmed and sliced
- ¾ cup white wine, preferably Chardonnay
- 2 pounds wild-caught salmon fillet, skinned, cut into 6 portions
- 14 large cloves garlic, divided
- ¼ cup extra-virgin olive oil
- 2 tablespoons finely chopped fresh oregano, divided
- Lemon wedges

Directions:

1. Preheat oven to 450 degrees F.
2. Mince 2 garlic cloves and combine in a small bowl with oil, 1 tablespoon oregano, 1/2 teaspoon salt and 1/4 teaspoon pepper.
3. Halve the remaining 37 garlic and toss with Brussels sprouts and 3 tablespoons of the seasoned oil in a large roasting pan. Roast, stirring once, for 15 minutes.
4. Add wine to the remaining oil mixture. Remove the pan from oven, stir the vegetables and place salmon on top. Drizzle with the wine mixture.
5. Sprinkle with the remaining 1 tablespoon oregano and 1/2 teaspoon each salt and pepper.
6. Bake until the salmon is just cooked through, 5 to 10 minutes more. Serve with lemon wedges.

Easy Salmon Cakes With Arugula Salad

Ingredients:

- ½ teaspoon ground pepper, divided
- ½ cup panko breadcrumbs
- ½ cup crème fraîche or sour cream
- ¼ cup buttermilk
- 3 tablespoons chopped fresh dill
- ½ teaspoon salt, divided
- 2 tablespoons extra-virgin olive oil
- 1 (5 ounce) package arugula
- 1 pound salmon, preferably wild, skinned
- 2 tablespoons lemon juice, divided
- 2 teaspoons Dijon mustard, divided

- ½ cup finely chopped yellow bell pepper
- 1 tablespoon finely chopped shallot
- 1 cup sliced radishes

Directions:

1. Coarsely chop salmon and place half in a food processor.
2. Add 1 tablespoon lemon juice and 1 teaspoon mustard. Process, scraping down the sides as necessary, until smooth.
3. Add the remaining salmon, bell pepper, shallot and 1/4 teaspoon pepper and pulse until the mixture is combined but still chunky.
4. Transfer the salmon mixture to a medium bowl.
5. Add breadcrumbs and stir until combined. Form the salmon into 4 patties, about 4 inches wide each, and place on a plate. Freeze for 5 minutes.

6. Meanwhile, whisk crème fraîche (or sour cream), buttermilk, dill and 1/4 teaspoon salt with the remaining 1 tablespoon lemon juice, 1 teaspoon mustard and 1/4 teaspoon pepper in a large bowl.
7. Set aside 1/4 cup of the dressing for drizzling.
8. Heat oil in a large cast-iron or nonstick skillet over medium-high heat.
9. Add the salmon cakes and cook, flipping once, until well browned and cooked through, 2 to 3 minutes per side.
10. Transfer to a clean plate and sprinkle with the remaining 1/4 teaspoon salt.
11. Add arugula and radishes to the dressing in the large bowl. Toss to coat.
12. Serve the salmon cakes on top of the salad, drizzled with the reserved 1/4 cup dressing.

Broccoli & Cauliflower Casserole

Ingredients:

- 2 cups whole milk
- 2 ounces reduced-fat cream cheese, at room temperature
- 1 teaspoon garlic powder
- 1 teaspoon onion powder
- ½ teaspoon ground pepper
- ¼ teaspoon salt
- 1 cup shredded sharp white Cheddar cheese
- ¾ cup panko breadcrumbs
- 1 (2 pound) head cauliflower, trimmed and cut into 1-inch florets
- 1 pound broccoli florets, cut into 1-inch pieces

- ¼ cup unsalted butter, divided

- 2 tablespoons all-purpose flour

- ¼ cup grated Parmesan cheese

Directions:

1. Preheat oven to 375°F. Coat a 2-quart baking dish with cooking spray; set aside.
2. Add 1 inch of water to a large stockpot fitted with a steamer basket; cover and bring to boil.
3. Add cauliflower florets first, then top with broccoli florets; steam, covered, until slightly tender, about 6 minutes.
4. Remove the vegetables from the pot; set aside. Discard the water and clean the pot.
5. Heat 2 tablespoons butter in the pot over medium heat. Add flour and cook, stirring constantly, until nutty, about 1 minute.
6. Gradually stir in milk, whisking constantly, until simmering. Whisk in cream cheese, garlic powder, onion powder, pepper and salt.

7. Cook, whisking constantly, until thickened and smooth, about 2 minutes. Reduce
8. heat to low and gradually add Cheddar, whisking until melted after each addition. Remove from heat.
9. Add the broccoli and cauliflower to the sauce and stir to coat. Transfer to the prepared baking dish.
10. Microwave the remaining 2 tablespoons butter in a medium microwaveable bowl on High until melted, about 25 seconds.
11. Stir in panko and Parmesan until fully coated; sprinkle evenly over the casserole.
12. Bake until golden brown and bubbly, 25 to 30 minutes. Let stand for 5 minutes before serving.

Grilled Chicken With Roasted Vegetables

Ingredients:

- 1 teaspoon dried oregano
- 1 teaspoon dried basil
- 1 teaspoon salt
- 1/2 teaspoon pepper
- 1 large onion, sliced into wedges
- 2 large carrots, sliced into 1/2-inch thick slices
- 2 red bell peppers, cut into strips
- 2 lbs boneless, skinless chicken breasts
- 2 tablespoons olive oil
- 1 teaspoon garlic powder
- 2 zucchinis, sliced into 1/4-inch thick slices

Directions:
1. Preheat a grill to medium-high heat.
2. In a large bowl, combine the olive oil, garlic powder, oregano, basil, salt and pepper. Add the chicken and stir to coat.
3. Place the onion, carrots, bell peppers and zucchini on a large baking sheet. Drizzle with olive oil and sprinkle with salt and pepper. Toss to coat.
4. Grill the chicken for 4-5 minutes per side, until cooked through.
5. Place the vegetables on the grill and cook for 5-7 minutes per side, until tender and lightly charred.
6. Serve the grilled chicken with the roasted vegetables. Enjoy!

Chicken And Rice Soup

Ingredients:

- 2 – 3 cups cooked chicken, shredded or diced
- 2 teaspoons dried thyme
- 6 – 8 cups chicken broth
- 1/2 cup long grain white rice
- 1/4 cup fresh parsley, chopped
- 2 tablespoons olive oil
- 1 medium onion, diced
- 2 cloves garlic, minced
- 2 carrots, peeled and diced
- 2 stalks celery, diced
- Salt and pepper to taste

Directions:

1. Heat olive oil in a large pot over medium heat.
2. Add onions and garlic and cook for 2 minutes.
3. Add the carrots and celery and cook for another 3 minutes.
4. Add the chicken, thyme, and chicken broth and bring to a boil.
5. Reduce heat to low and add the rice. Simmer for 20 minutes.
6. Add the parsley, salt, and pepper and simmer for another 5 minutes.
7. Serve the soup warm with crusty bread. Enjoy!

Herb-Crusted Baked Chicken

Ingredients:

- 1 teaspoon dried thyme
- 1 teaspoon paprika
- 1/2 teaspoon salt
- 1/4 teaspoon ground pepper
- 2 large eggs, lightly beaten
- 1/2 cup plain breadcrumbs
- 2 tablespoons chopped fresh parsley
- 4 boneless and skinless chicken breasts
- 1/2 cup all-purpose flour
- 1 teaspoon garlic powder
- 1 teaspoon dried oregano

- 1 teaspoon dried basil

- 2 tablespoons butter, melted

Directions:
1. Preheat oven to 375 degrees F. Grease a 9x13 inch baking dish.
2. In a shallow bowl, mix together the flour, garlic powder, oregano, basil, thyme, paprika, salt, and pepper.
3. In a separate shallow bowl, beat the eggs.
4. In a third shallow bowl, mix together the breadcrumbs and parsley.
5. Dip each chicken breast in the flour mixture, then in the beaten eggs, and finally in the breadcrumb mixture. Place the chicken breasts in the prepared baking dish.
6. Drizzle the melted butter over the chicken breasts.
7. Bake for 20 minutes, or until chicken is cooked through and golden brown. Serve warm.

Lemon Garlic Shrimp Stir-Fry

Ingredients:

- 2 minced garlic cloves
- Two teaspoons of lemon juice, fresh
- 1 cup of snap peas; 1 red bell pepper, sliced; 1 yellow bell pepper, sliced; 1
- Zucchini, sliced
- Pepper and salt as desired
- 1 pound of peeled and deveined shrimp
- Olive oil, two tablespoons
- Chopped fresh cilantro (for decoration)

Directions:

1. Warm up the olive oil in a sizable skillet or wok over medium-high heat.

2. When aromatic, add the minced garlic and cook for one minute.
3. When the shrimp are pink and opaque, add them to the skillet and simmer for 2–3 minutes. The shrimp should be taken out of the skillet and put aside.
4. Add the zucchini, snap peas, and red and yellow bell peppers in the same skillet.
5. Vegetables should be stir-fried for 4-5 minutes or until crisp-tender.
6. Add fresh lemon juice to the skillet where the cooked shrimp was first placed. To taste, add salt and pepper to the food.
7. To blend the flavors, stir everything together for an additional minute.
8. Serve the lemon garlic shrimp stir-fry as a tasty and eye-catching seafood dish with fresh cilantro cut for garnish.

Baked Lemon Dijon Salmon

Ingredients:

- Two teaspoons of lemon juice, fresh
- Olive oil, 1 tbsp
- 1 tablespoon finely sliced fresh dill
- Pepper and salt as desired
- 4 fillets of salmon
- Dijon mustard, two tablespoons

Directions:
1. A baking sheet should be lined with parchment paper and the oven should be preheated to 400°F (200°C).
2. Mix the Dijon mustard, lemon juice, olive oil, minced dill, salt, and pepper in a small bowl.

3. The salmon fillets should be placed on the prepared baking sheet.
4. Each salmon fillet should be evenly coated with the mustard mixture by being brushed over the top.
5. Bake the salmon for 12 to 15 minutes, or until it is cooked through and flakes easily.
6. With a side of roasted vegetables or a crisp salad, serve the baked salmon with lemon and Dijon sauce.

Shrimp With Spicy Garlic

Ingredients:

- 4 minced garlic cloves
- One teaspoon of red pepper flakes, tasted,
- 2 teaspoons chopped fresh parsley
- Pepper and salt as desired
- 1 pound of peeled and deveined shrimp
- Olive oil, two tablespoons
- Slices of lemon (for serving)

Directions:

1. Over medium heat, warm the olive oil in a large skillet.
2. Red pepper flakes and minced garlic are added to the skillet. Sauté until fragrant for one minute.

3. Salt and pepper the shrimp before adding them to the skillet. Cook the shrimp for 2 to 3 minutes, or until they are opaque and pink.
4. Toss cooked shrimp with fresh parsley after sprinkling it on top.
5. Serve the hot garlic shrimp with lemon wedges on the side for squeezing.

Lentil And Vegetable Curry

Ingredients:

- 1 red bell pepper, diced
- 1 zucchini, diced
- 1 tablespoon curry powder
- 1 teaspoon ground cumin
- 1/4 teaspoon cayenne pepper (optional)
- 1 can (14 ounces) diced tomatoes
- 1 cup dried green lentils, rinsed and drained
- 2 cups low-FODMAP vegetable broth
- 1 tablespoon olive oil
- 1 medium carrot, diced
- Salt and pepper to taste

- Chopped fresh cilantro for garnish

Directions:
1. In a saucepan, combine the lentils and vegetable broth. Bring to a boil.
2. Reduce heat to low, cover, and simmer for about 20-25 minutes or until the lentils are tender.
3. In a separate pan, heat olive oil over medium heat.
4. Add the diced carrot, red bell pepper, and zucchini. Sauté for about 5-6 minutes or until the vegetables are slightly softened.
5. Add the curry powder, ground cumin, and cayenne pepper (if using) to the pan. Stir for 1 minute to toast the spices.
6. Pour in the diced tomatoes and cooked lentils with their broth.
7. Season with salt and pepper. Simmer for another 10-15 minutes to allow the flavors to meld together.

8. Serve hot, garnished with chopped fresh cilantro.

Quinoa Breakfast Bowl

Ingredients:

- 1 tablespoon chia seeds
- 1 tablespoon unsweetened shredded coconut
- 1/4 cup sliced almonds
- 1 cup cooked quinoa
- 1 cup lactose-free milk (such as almond or rice milk)
- 1 tablespoon maple syrup
- 1/4 cup fresh berries (e.g., blueberries, raspberries)

Directions:

1. In a saucepan, warm the lactose-free milk over medium heat.

2. Stir in the cooked quinoa, maple syrup, chia seeds, shredded coconut, and sliced almonds.
3. Cook for about 5 minutes, stirring occasionally, until heated through.
4. Divide the quinoa mixture into bowls.
5. Top with fresh berries.
6. Serve warm.

Greek Salad

Ingredients:

- 1/4 cup sliced Kalamata olives
- 1/4 cup crumbled lactose-free feta cheese (optional)
- 2 tablespoons extra-virgin olive oil
- 1 tablespoon fresh lemon juice
- 1/2 teaspoon dried oregano
- 2 cups mixed salad greens
- 1 cucumber, sliced
- 1/2 cup cherry tomatoes, halved
- Salt and pepper to taste

Directions:

1. In a salad bowl, combine the mixed greens, cucumber slices, cherry tomatoes, Kalamata olives, and crumbled lactose-free feta cheese (if using).
2. In a small bowl, whisk together the olive oil, lemon juice, dried oregano, salt, and pepper to make the dressing.
3. Drizzle the dressing over the salad.
4. Toss gently to coat all the Ingredients: evenly.
5. Serve immediately.

Pasta Salad

Ingredients:

- 1/2 cup red bell pepper, diced
- 1/4 cup kalamata olives, pitted and sliced
- 1/4 cup feta cheese, crumbled
- Low FODMAP dressing (recipe below)
- 8 ounces low FODMAP pasta (such as quinoa pasta, lentil pasta, or chickpea pasta)
- 1 cup cucumber, diced
- 1/2 cup cherry tomatoes, quartered
- Salt and pepper to taste

Low fodmap dressing:

- 1 teaspoon honey

- 1/2 teaspoon dried oregano
- 1/4 teaspoon salt
- 1/4 cup olive oil
- 2 tablespoons red wine vinegar
- 1 tablespoon Dijon mustard
- 1/4 teaspoon black pepper

Directions:

1. The pasta should be prepared as directed on the packaging. Drain and coolly rinse with cold water.
2. Combine the spaghetti, cucumber, tomatoes, bell pepper, olives, and feta cheese in a sizable bowl.
3. Mix the olive oil, red wine vinegar, Dijon mustard, honey, oregano, salt, and pepper in a small bowl.
4. Toss the pasta salad with the dressing after pouring it over it.
5. To taste, add salt and pepper to the food.
6. Serve right away or chill in the fridge until you're ready to.

Chicken Wrap

Ingredients:

- 1/2 cup shredded lettuce
- 1/4 cup sliced cucumber
- 1/4 cup sliced red bell pepper
- 2 tablespoons chopped fresh cilantro
- 1 tablespoon mayonnaise
- 1 tablespoon Dijon mustard
- 1 boneless, skinless chicken breast
- 1 tablespoon olive oil
- Salt and pepper to taste
- Gluten-free tortilla or wrap

Directions:

1. Set the grill or grill pan on the stove to medium heat.
2. Add salt and pepper to the chicken breast before cooking. Olive oil should be applied on both sides of the chicken and then rubbed in.
3. Cook the chicken breast on the prepared grill for 6 to 8 minutes on each side, or until it is thoroughly cooked and the middle is no longer pink. Slice after removing from the grill and giving it some time to rest.
4. Prepare the vegetables while the chicken cooks. The red bell pepper and cucumber should be sliced into thin strips, and the fresh cilantro should be chopped.
5. The mayonnaise and Dijon mustard should be thoroughly mixed in a small bowl.
6. If necessary, reheat the gluten-free tortilla or wrap in accordance with the directions on the packaging.

7. Spread the mayo and Dijon mustard mixture equally over the tortilla or wrap before assembling it.
8. The center of the tortilla or wrap should be filled with the chopped cilantro, red bell pepper strips, sliced cucumber, and shreds of lettuce.
9. Place cooked chicken breast on top of the vegetables after slicing it into thin strips.
10. To enclose the filling, carefully fold the sides of the tortilla or wrap in. Then, roll it up securely from one end to the other.
11. Serve the wrap right away after cutting it in half diagonally.

Ground Beef Tacos

Ingredients:

- 1 pound lean ground beef (or ground turkey)
- 1 (4-ounce) can diced mild green chilies, undrained
- ¼ cup water
- 2 tablespoons tomato paste
- 1 teaspoon ground cumin
- 1 teaspoon smoked paprika
- 2 teaspoons garlic-infused olive oil
- Salt and black pepper to taste
- Corn tortillas
- Your favorite taco toppings (shredded cheese, lettuce, tomatoes, sour cream, etc.)

Directions:

1. Over medium heat, warm the olive oil in a large skillet.
2. When the ground beef is added, brown it while breaking it up with a spatula. Get rid of any extra fat.
3. Add the tomato paste, water, cumin, paprika, salt, and pepper after incorporating the diced green chilies.
4. Cook for 5 minutes, or until the sauce has thickened, after bringing to a simmer.
5. The corn tortillas should be warmed as directed on the packaging.
6. Fill a portion of the ground beef mixture into each tortilla before adding your preferred toppings to complete the tacos.

Low Fodmap Sandwich

Ingredients:

- 1/4 cup low FODMAP protein, such as grilled chicken, salmon, or tofu

- 1/4 cup low FODMAP vegetables, such as lettuce, tomato, and cucumber

- 2 slices low FODMAP bread

- 1 tablespoon low FODMAP mayonnaise or mustard (optional)

Directions:
1. Spread the mayonnaise or mustard on one slice of bread.
2. Layer the protein, vegetables, and other slice of bread on top.
3. Cut the sandwich in half and serve.

Low Fodmap Wrap

Ingredients:

- 1/4 cup low FODMAP vegetables, such as lettuce, tomato, and cucumber
- 1 tablespoon low FODMAP hummus or salsa
- 1 low FODMAP tortilla
- 1/4 cup low FODMAP protein, such as grilled chicken, salmon, or tofu

Directions:
1. Spread the hummus or salsa on the tortilla.
2. Layer the protein, vegetables, and other Ingredients: on top.
3. Roll up the tortilla and cut it in half.
4. Serve immediately.

Grilled Steak With Roasted Potatoes

Ingredients:

- Potatoes
- Garlic-infused olive oil
- Fresh rosemary
- Steak (such as sirloin or ribeye)
- Salt and pepper

Directions:

1. Preheat the grill or broiler.
2. Cut potatoes into wedges.
3. Toss the potato wedges with garlic-infused olive oil, fresh rosemary, salt, and pepper.
4. Place the potato wedges on a baking sheet and roast in the oven until golden and crispy.
5. Season the steak with salt and pepper.
6. Grill or broil the steak to desired doneness.

7. Allow the steak to rest for some minutes before slicing.
8. Serve the grilled steak with roasted potatoes and a side of steamed vegetables.

Capers Salad

Ingredients:

- Fresh basil leaves
- Balsamic vinegar
- Olive oil
- Tomato
- Mozzarella cheese (lactose-free if necessary)
- Salt and pepper

Directions:

1. Slice tomatoes and mozzarella cheese into rounds.
2. Arrange the tomato and mozzarella slices on a plate, alternating.
3. Place fresh basil leaves between the slices.

4. Drizzle balsamic vinegar and olive oil over the salad.
5. Season with salt and pepper.
6. Serve the low FODMAP Caprese salad as a light appetizer or side dish.

Lemon Herb Roasted Chicken Thighs

Ingredients:

- Lemon
- Fresh herbs (such as thyme or rosemary)
- Garlic-infused olive oil
- Chicken thighs
- Salt and pepper

Directions:
1. Preheat the oven to 425°F (220°C).
2. Pat dry the chicken thighs.
3. Drizzle garlic-infused olive oil over the chicken thighs.
4. Squeeze lemon juice over the thighs.
5. Sprinkle with fresh herbs, salt, and pepper.
6. On a baking sheet with parchment paper, spread out the chicken thighs.

7. Bake for about 25-30 minutes or until the chicken is cooked through and golden.
8. Serve the lemon herb roasted chicken thighs with a side of roasted vegetables or a salad.

www.ingramcontent.com/pod-product-compliance
Lightning Source LLC
LaVergne TN
LVHW010222070526
838199LV00062B/4693